THE BEATLES
FOR ACCORDION

Arrangements by Gary Meisner

Cover photo by Michael Ochs Archives/Getty Images

ISBN 978-1-5400-2427-5

Visit Hal Leonard Online at
www.halleonard.com

Contact Us:
Hal Leonard
7777 West Bluemound Road
Milwaukee, WI 53213
Email: info@halleonard.com

In Europe contact:
Hal Leonard Europe Limited
Distribution Centre, Newmarket Road
Bury St Edmunds, Suffolk, IP33 3YB
Email: info@halleonardeurope.com

In Australia contact:
Hal Leonard Australia Pty. Ltd.
4 Lentara Court
Cheltenham, Victoria, 3192 Australia
Email: info@halleonard.com.au

ALL MY LOVING

Words and Music by JOHN LENNON
and PAUL McCARTNEY

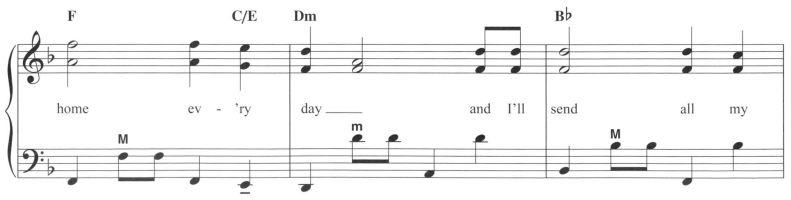

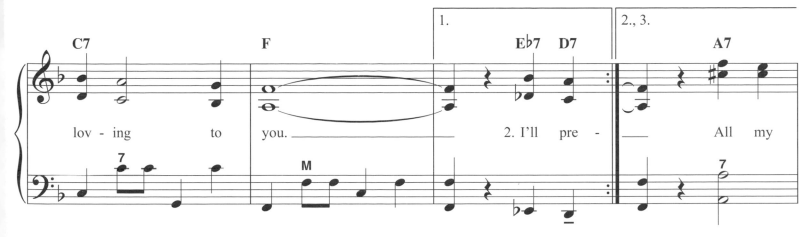

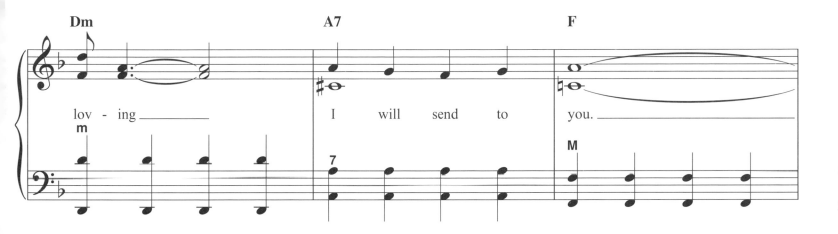

4

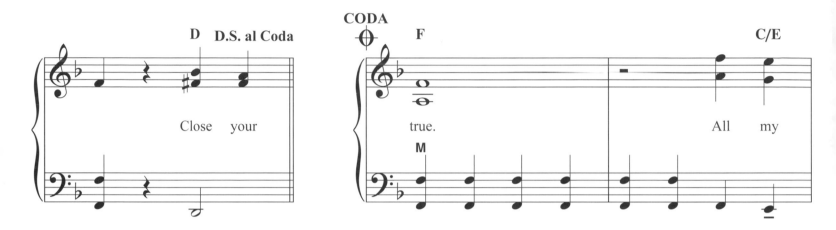

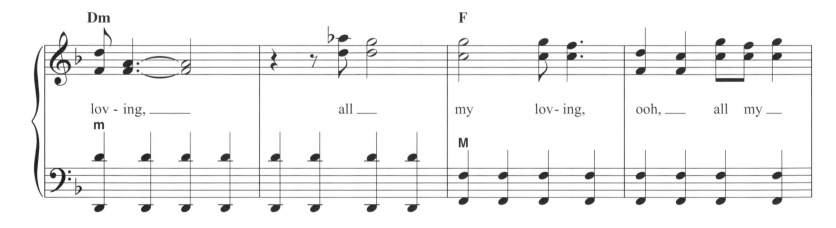

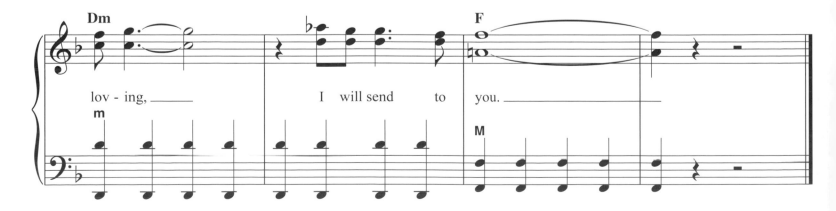

ALL YOU NEED IS LOVE

Words and Music by JOHN LENNON
and PAUL McCARTNEY

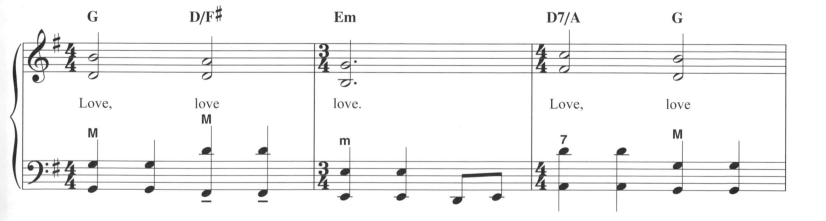

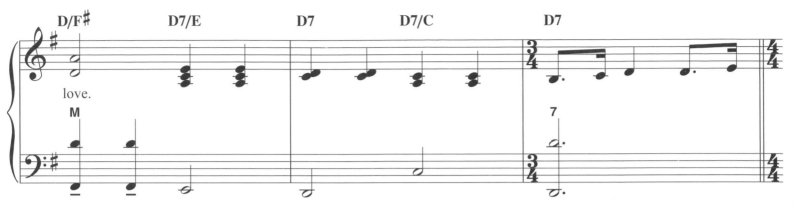

love.

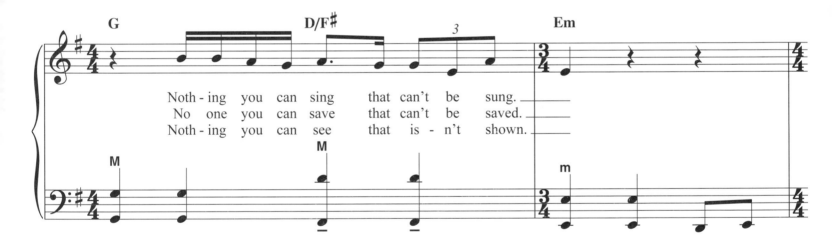

There's noth-ing you can do that can't be done. _
There's noth-ing you can make that can't be made. _
There's noth-ing you can know that is-n't known. _

Noth-ing you can sing that can't be sung. _
No one you can save that can't be saved. _
Noth-ing you can see that is-n't shown. _

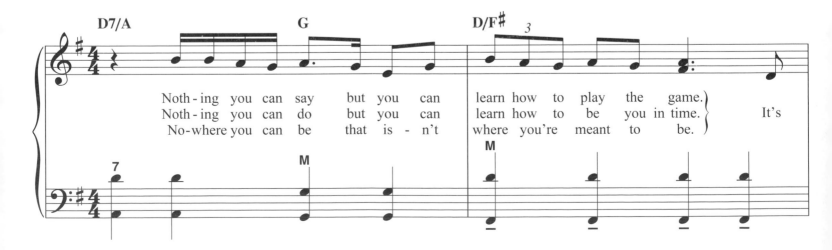

Noth-ing you can say but you can learn how to play the game. }
Noth-ing you can do but you can learn how to be you in time. } It's
No-where you can be that is-n't where you're meant to be. }

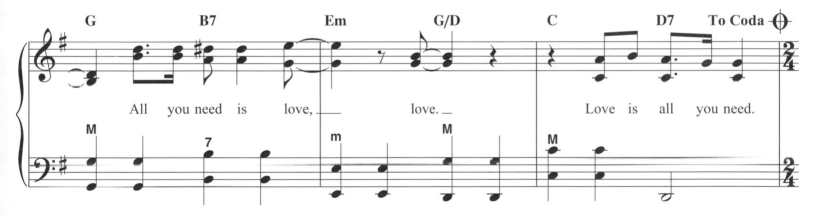

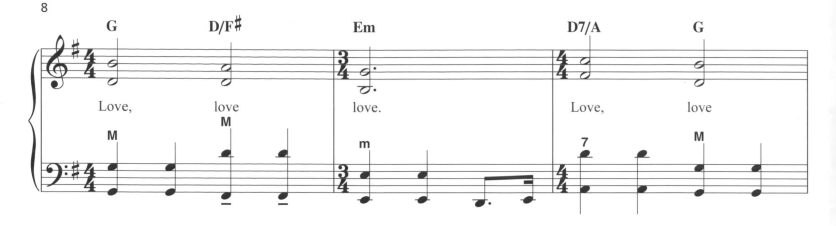

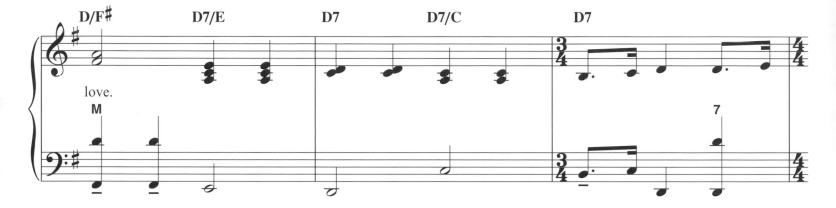

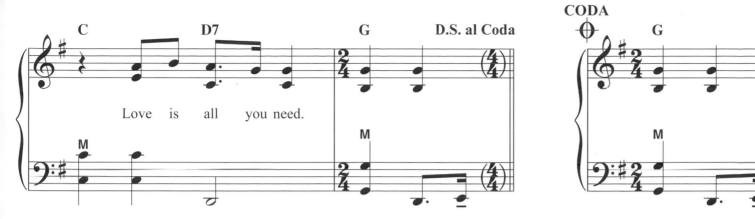

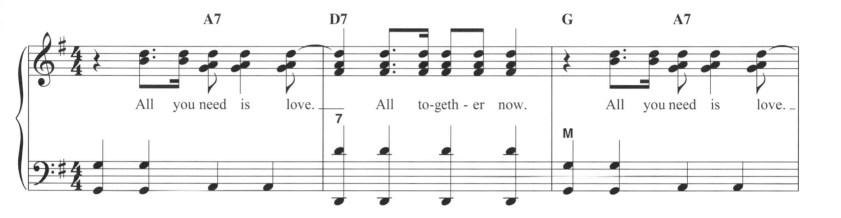

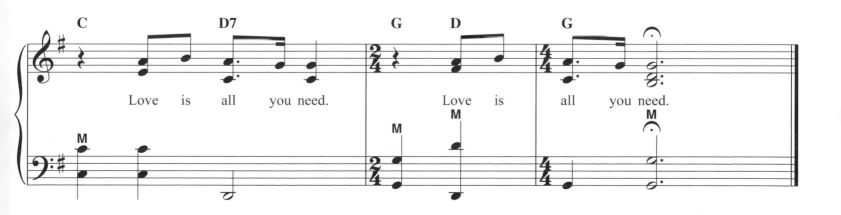

AND I LOVE HER

Words and Music by JOHN LENNON
and PAUL McCARTNEY

I give her all ___ my love, ___ that's all I do. ___
She gives me ev - 'ry - thing ___ and ten - der - ly. ___
Bright are the stars ___ that shine, ___ dark is the sky. ___

And if you saw ___ my love, ___
The kiss my lov - er brings ___
I know this love ___ of mine ___

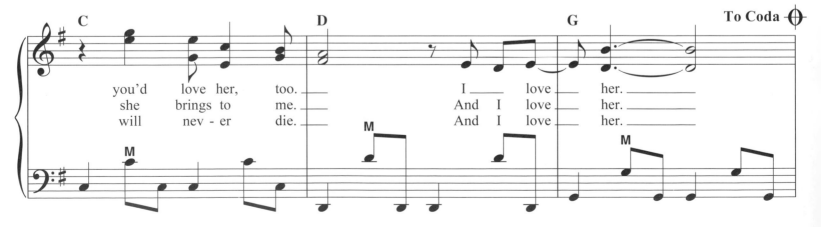

you'd love her, too. ___ I ___ love ___ her. ___
she brings to me. ___ And I love ___ her. ___
will nev - er die. ___ And I love ___ her. ___

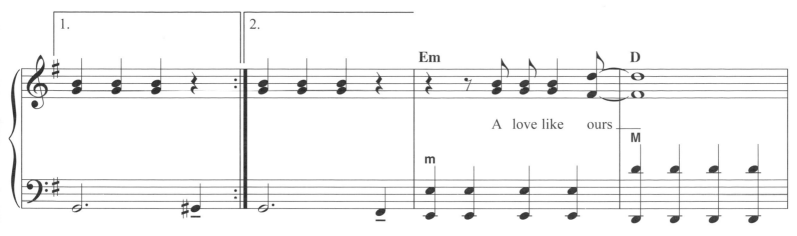

1. 2.

Em D

A love like ours

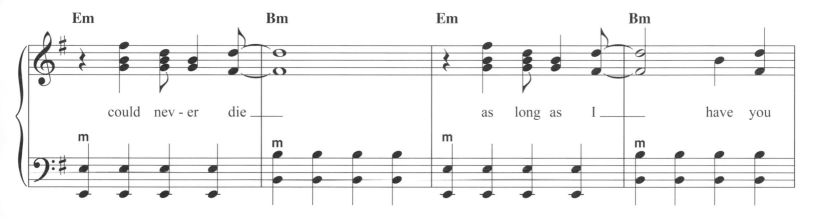

Em Bm Em Bm

could nev - er die   as long as I   have you

D D.S. al Coda CODA

near me.

Gm Dm Gm

(Instrumental)
Bright are the stars that shine,   dark is the

sky. _____ I know this love of mine _ will nev - er

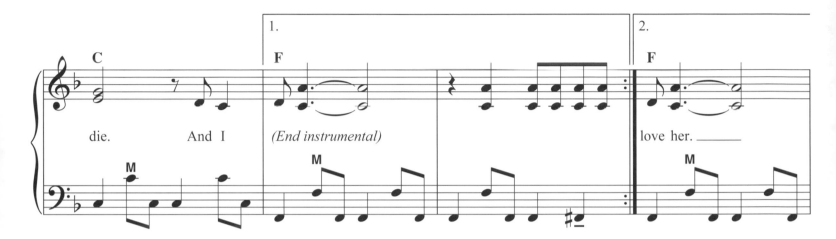

die. And I (End instrumental) love her. _____

THE FOOL ON THE HILL

Words and Music by JOHN LENNON
and PAUL McCARTNEY

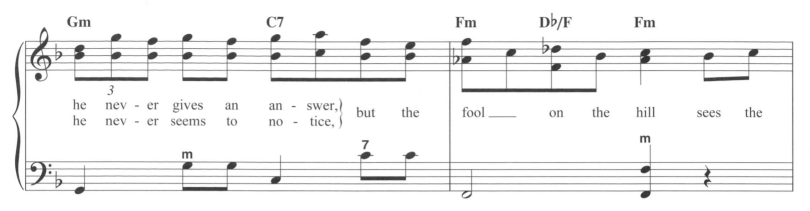

he nev - er gives an an - swer,
he nev - er seems to no - tice,
but the fool ___ on the hill sees the

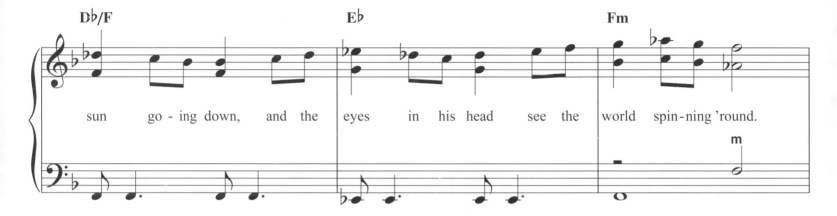

sun go - ing down, and the eyes in his head see the world spin-ning 'round.

(Instrumental)

No - bod - y seems to like him, they can tell what he wants to do, _____ and
He nev - er lis - tens to them, he knows that they're the fools, _____

he nev - er shows his feel - ings,⎫ but the fool _____ on the hill sees the
they don't like him, ⎭

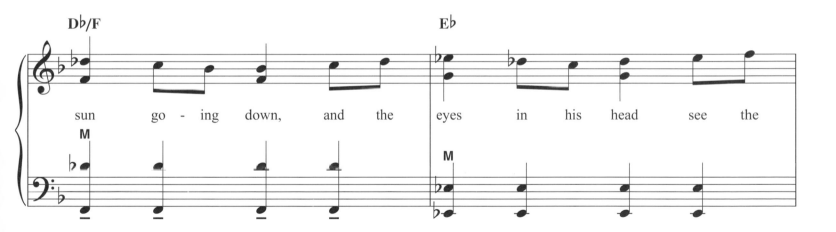

sun go - ing down, and the eyes in his head see the

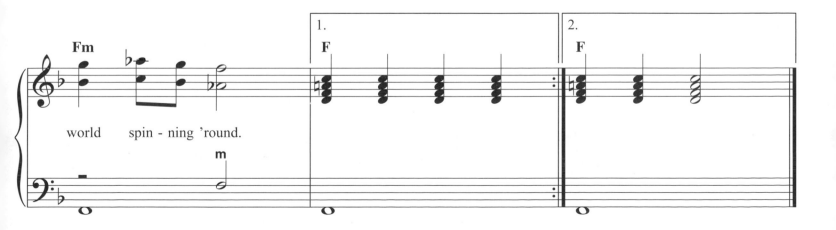

world spin - ning 'round.

ELEANOR RIGBY

Words and Music by JOHN LENNON
and PAUL McCARTNEY

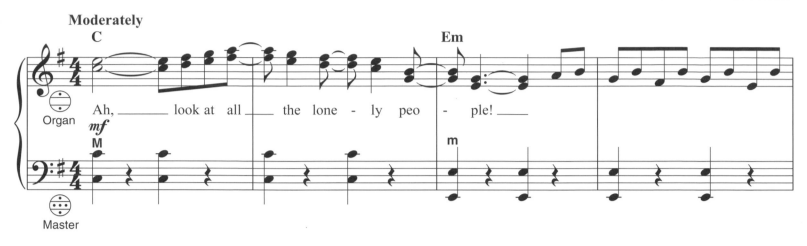

Ah, _____ look at all _____ the lone - ly peo - ple! _____

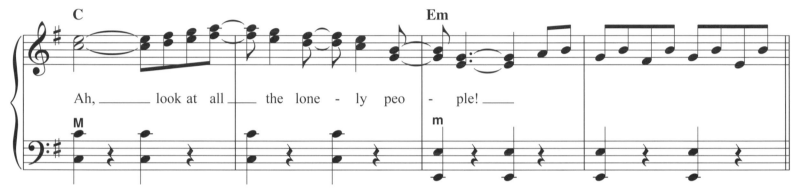

Ah, _____ look at all _____ the lone - ly peo - ple! _____

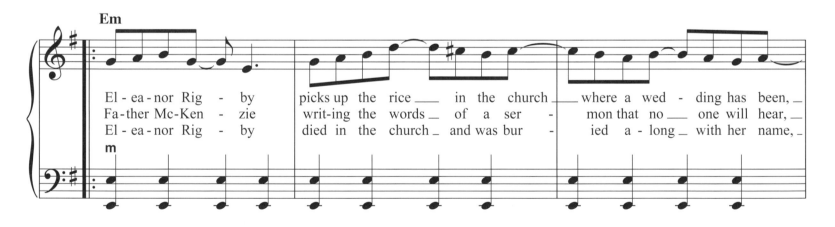

El - ea - nor Rig - by   picks up the rice _____ in the church _____ where a wed - ding has been, _____
Fa - ther Mc-Ken - zie   writ-ing the words _____ of a ser - mon that no _____ one will hear, _____
El - ea - nor Rig - by   died in the church _____ and was bur - ied a - long _____ with her name, _____

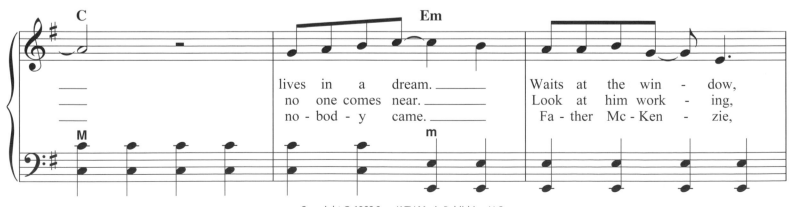

_____ lives in a dream. _____   Waits at the win - dow,
_____ no one comes near. _____   Look at him work - ing,
_____ no - bod - y came. _____   Fa - ther Mc - Ken - zie,

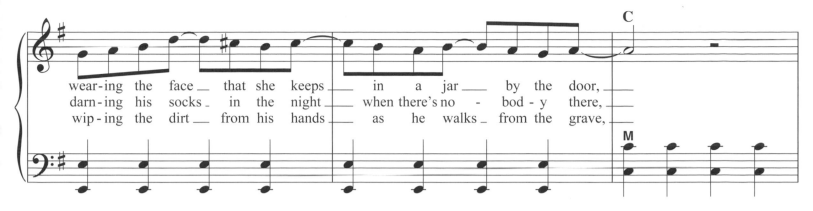

wear-ing the face ___ that she keeps ___ in a jar ___ by the door, ___
darn-ing his socks ___ in the night ___ when there's no - bod-y there, ___
wip-ing the dirt ___ from his hands ___ as he walks ___ from the grave,

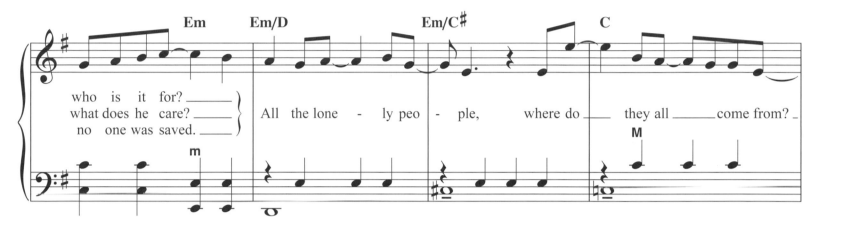

who is it for? ___
what does he care? ___
no one was saved. ___

All the lone - ly peo - ple, where do ___ they all ___ come from? ___

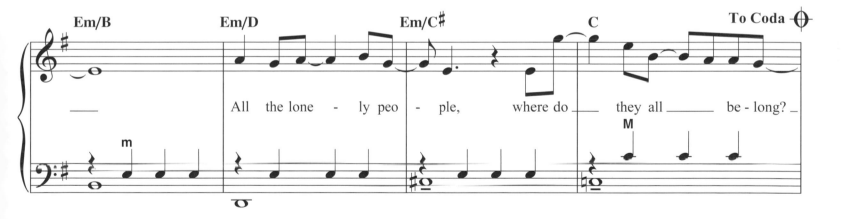

All the lone - ly peo - ple, where do ___ they all ___ be - long? ___

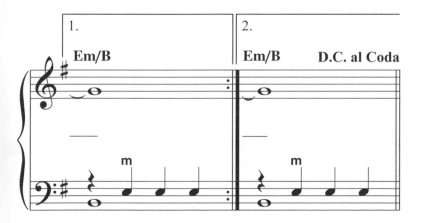

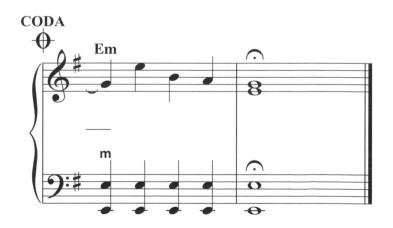

HERE COMES THE SUN

Words and Music by
GEORGE HARRISON

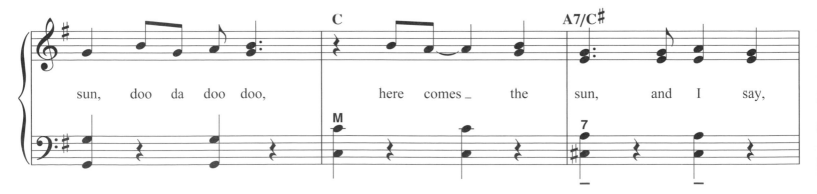

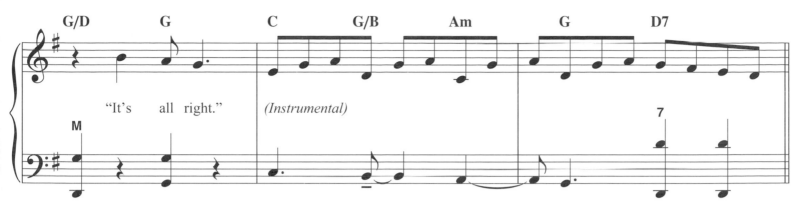

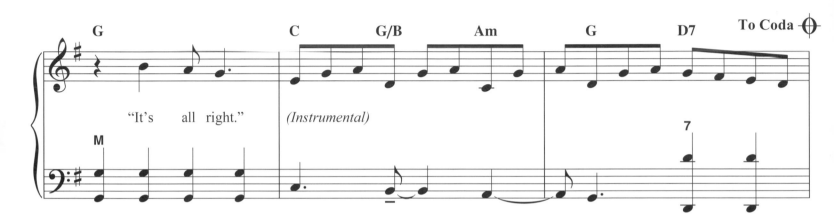

CODA

Here comes ___ the sun,   here comes ___ the

sun.   It's   all   right.   *(Instrumental)*

It's   all   right.   *(Instrumental)*

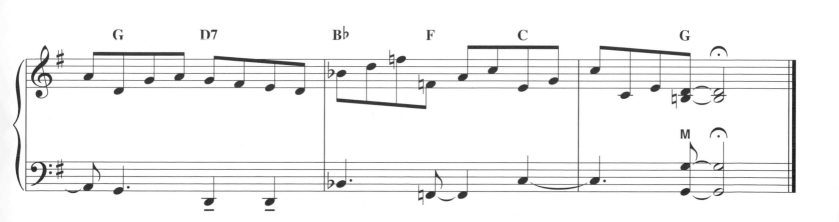

HERE, THERE AND EVERYWHERE

Words and Music by JOHN LENNON
and PAUL McCARTNEY

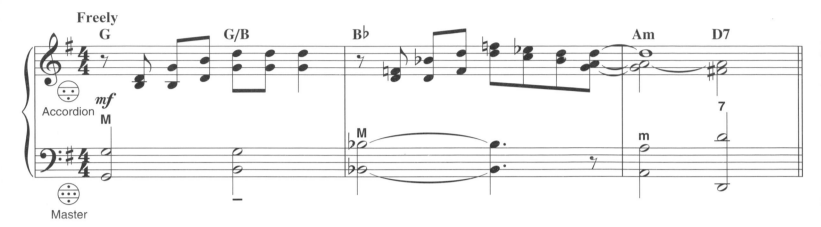

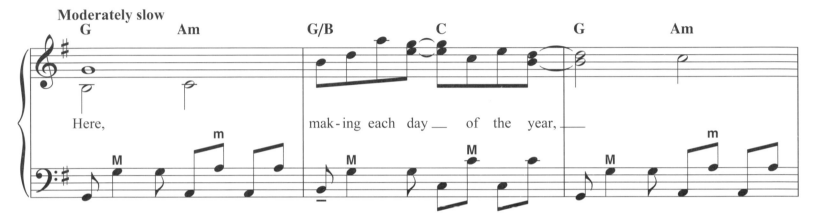

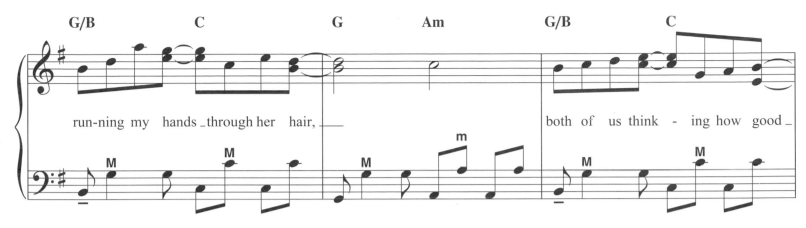

run-ning my hands _through her hair, ___ both of us think - ing how good_

___ it can be. ___ Some-one is speak - ing, but she does-n't know he's

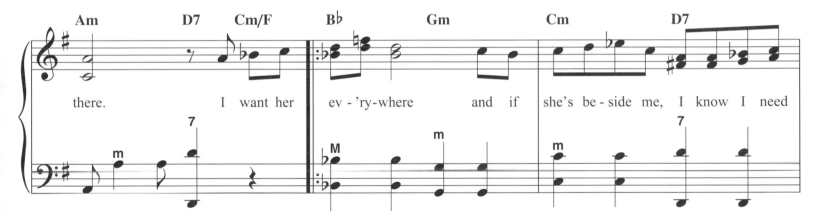

there. I want her ev - 'ry-where and if she's be-side me, I know I need

nev - er care. But to love her is to need her ev - 'ry-where,

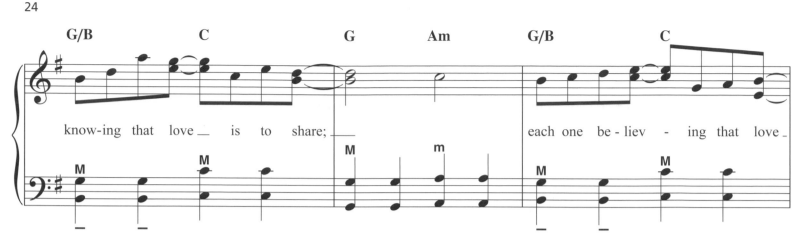

knowing that love __ is to share; __ each one believing that love __

__ never dies, __ watching her eyes __ and hoping I'm always

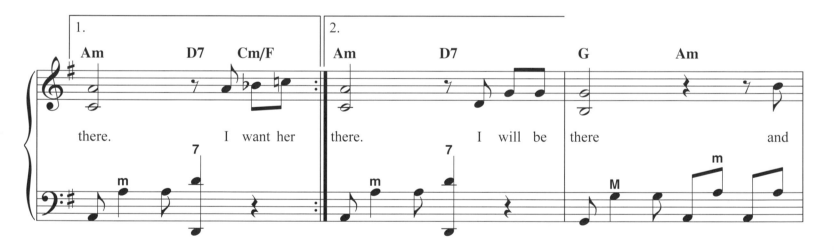

1. there. I want her
2. there. I will be there and

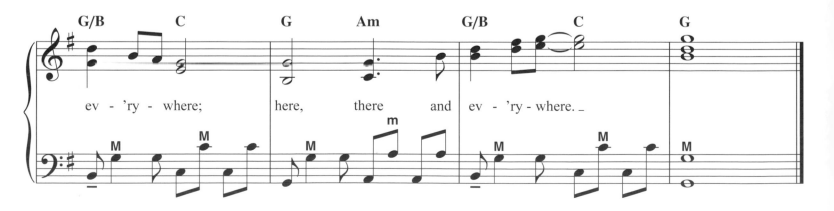

ev - 'ry - where; here, there and ev - 'ry - where. __

IN MY LIFE

Words and Music by JOHN LENNON
and PAUL McCARTNEY

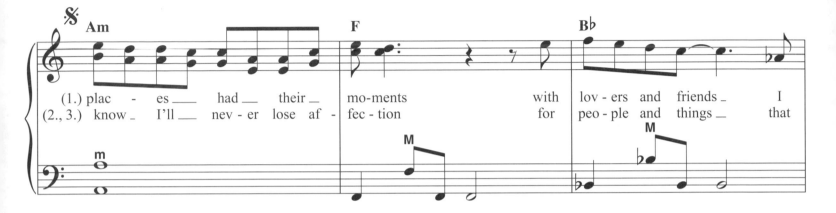

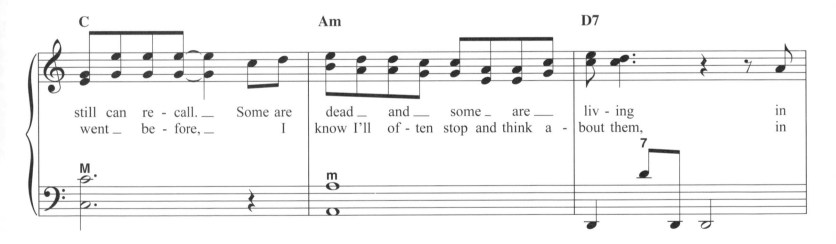

C   G7   Am   C7   F   Fm

(Instrumental)

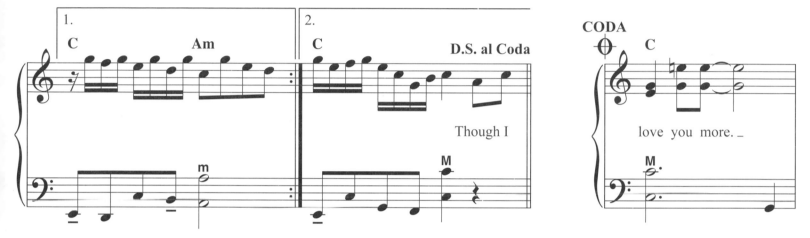

1.
C   Am

2.
C   D.S. al Coda

Though I

CODA
C

love you more.

G7   Fm

In my _____ life   I

N.C.   C   G7   C

love you   more.

HEY JUDE

Words and Music by JOHN LENNON
and PAUL McCARTNEY

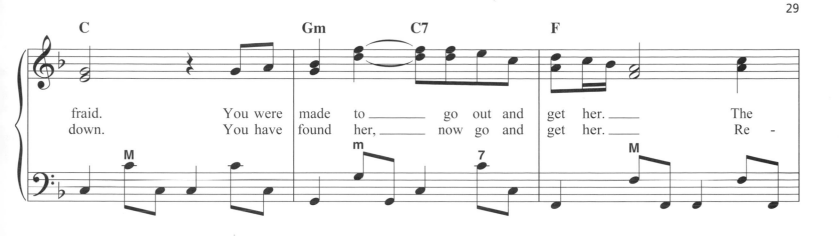

fraid. You were made to _____ go out and get her. _____ The
down. You have found her, _____ now go and get her. _____ Re -

min - ute you let her un - der your skin, then you be - gin _____
mem - ber to let her in - to your heart, then you can start _____

___ to make it _____ bet - ter. And an - y - time you feel the
___ to make it _____ bet - ter. So let it out and let it

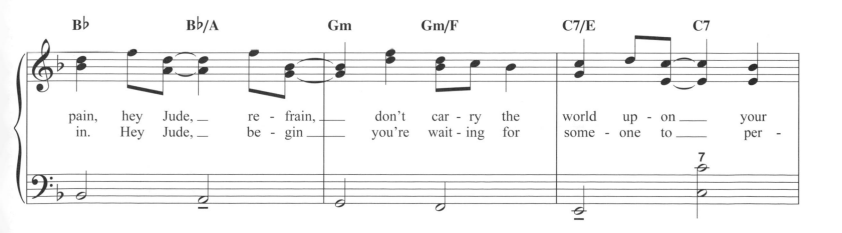

pain, hey Jude, ___ re - frain, ___ don't car - ry the world up - on ___ your
in. Hey Jude, ___ be - gin ___ you're wait - ing for some - one to ___ per -

shoul - ders. _\
form with. _\

For well you know that it's a   fool who plays _\ it cool _\
And don't you know that it's just   you, hey Jude, _\ you'll do. _\

___ by mak - ing his   world a lit - tle   cold - er. _____ Da da da
___ The move - ment you   need is on ___ your   shoul - der. _____

da ___ da da da da   da.   Hey ___

Hey ___   Jude, _____ don't make it bad,   take a

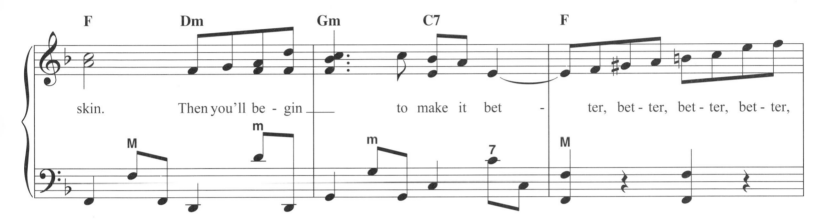

LET IT BE

Words and Music by JOHN LENNON
and PAUL McCARTNEY

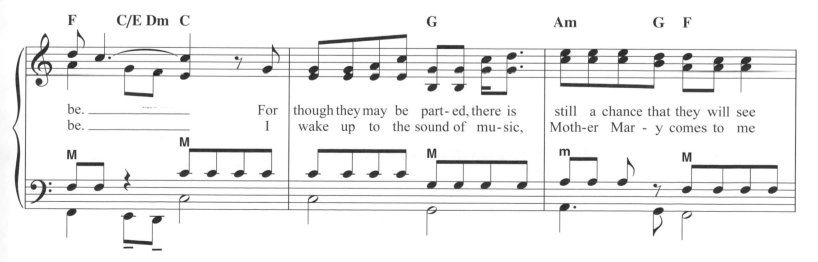

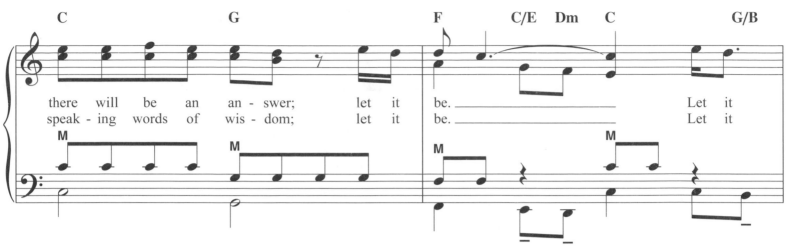

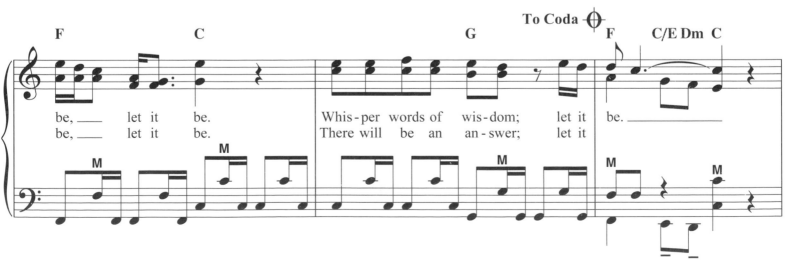

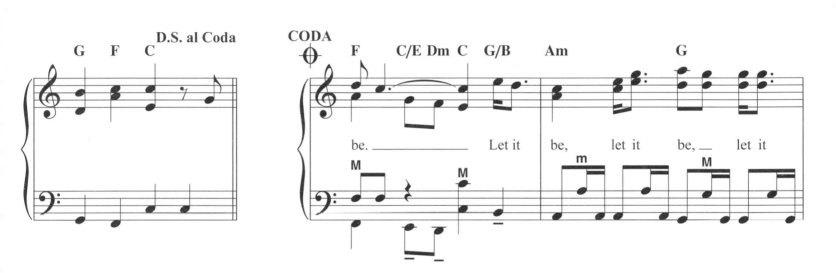

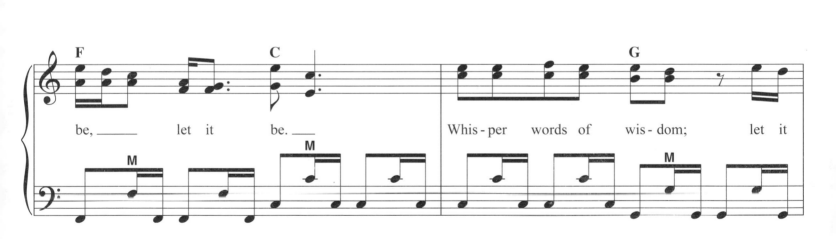

LUCY IN THE SKY WITH DIAMONDS

Words and Music by JOHN LENNON
and PAUL McCARTNEY

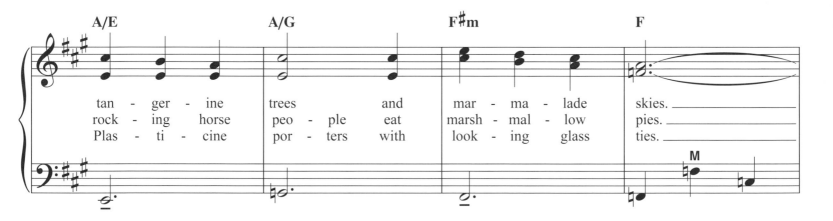

Pic - ture your - self in a boat on a riv - er, with
Fol - low her down to a bridge by a foun - tain, where
Pic - ture your - self on a train in a sta - tion, with

tan - ger - ine trees and mar - ma - lade skies.
rock - ing horse peo - ple eat marsh - mal - low pies.
Plas - ti - cine por - ters eat with look - ing glass ties.

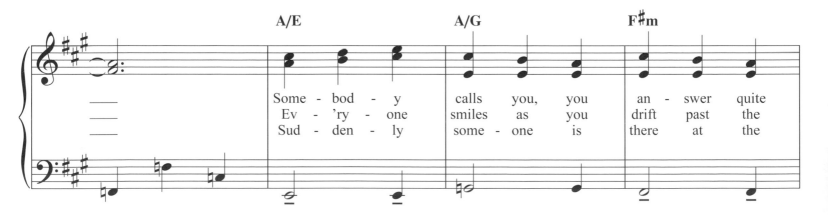

Some - bod - y calls you, you an - swer quite
Ev - 'ry - one smiles as you drift past the
Sud - den - ly some - one is there at the

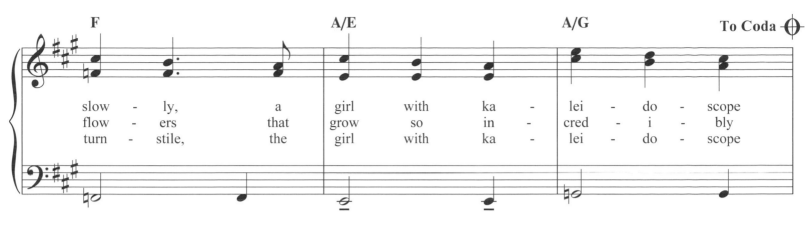

slow - ly, a girl with ka - lei - do - scope
flow - ers that grow so in - cred - i - bly
turn - stile, the girl with ka - lei - do - scope

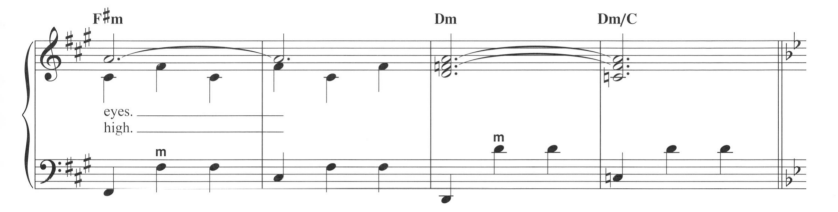

eyes.
high.

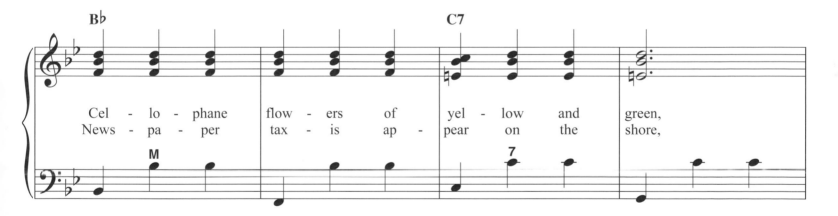

Cel - lo - phane flow - ers of yel - low and green,
News - pa - per tax - is ap - pear on the shore,

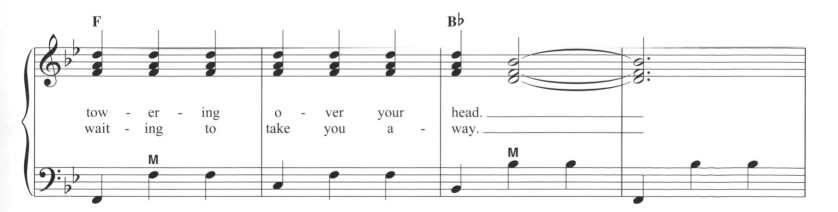

tow - er - ing o - ver your head.
wait - ing to take you a - way.

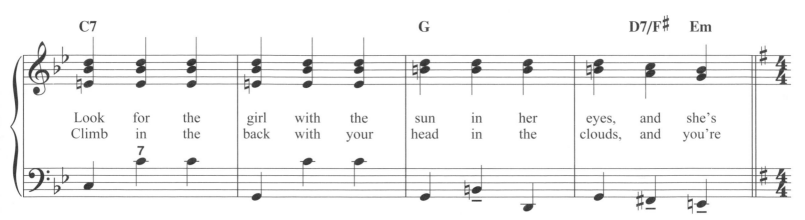

Look for the girl with the sun in her eyes, and she's
Climb in the back with your head in the clouds, and you're

Medium Rock

gone.)
gone.)

Lu - cy in the sky __ with dia - monds,

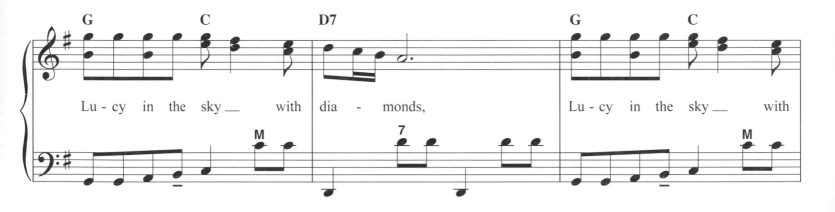

Lu - cy in the sky __ with dia - monds, Lu - cy in the sky __ with

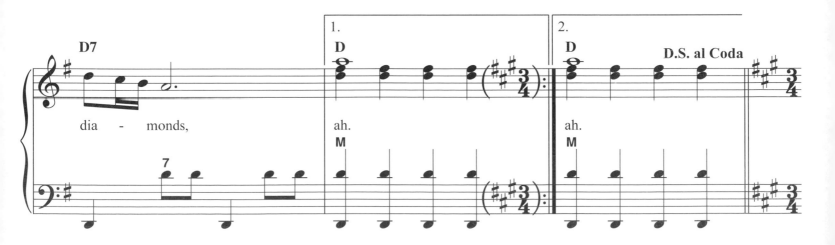

dia - monds,

1.
ah.

2.
ah. D.S. al Coda

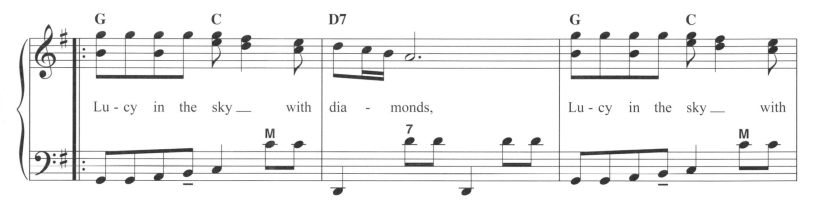

MICHELLE

Words and Music by JOHN LENNON
and PAUL McCARTNEY

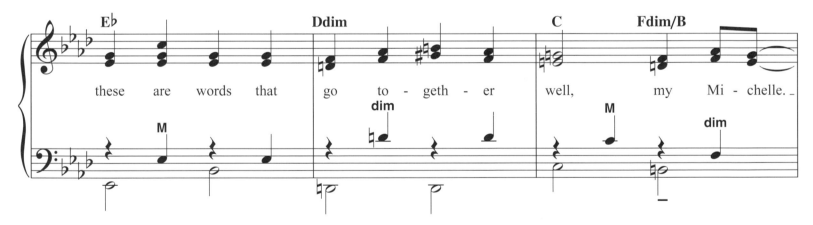

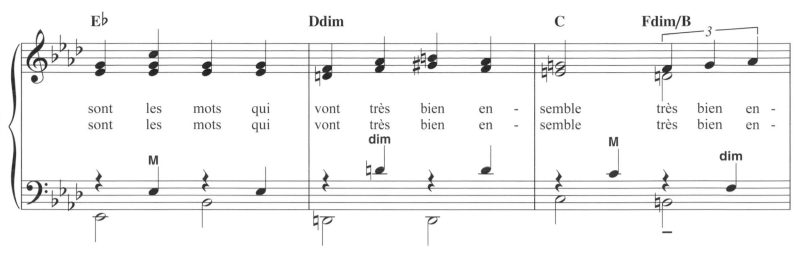

sont les mots qui vont très bien en - semble très bien en -
sont les mots qui vont très bien en - semble très bien en -

semble. I love you, I love you, I love you,
semble. I need to, I need to, I need to,

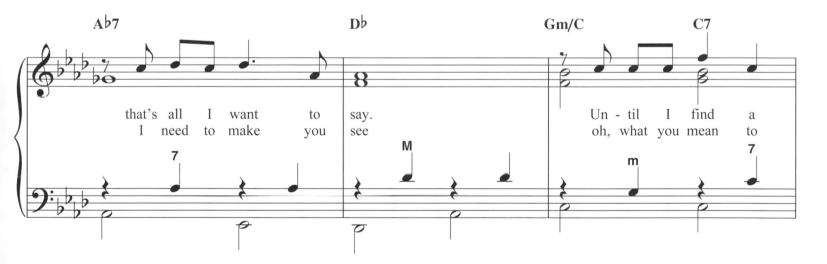

that's all I want to say. Un - til I find a
I need to make you see oh, what you mean to

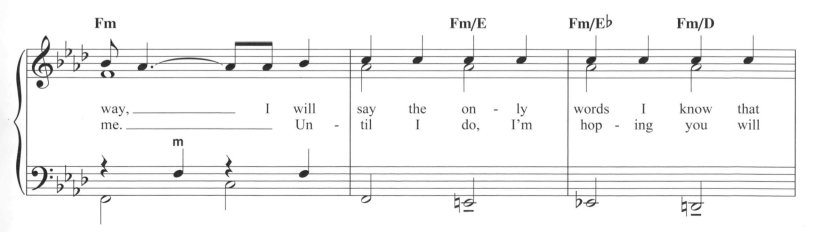

way, _____ I will say the on - ly words I know that
me. _____ Un - til I do, I'm hop - ing you will

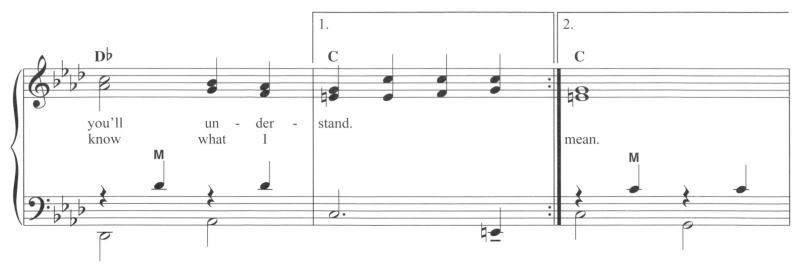

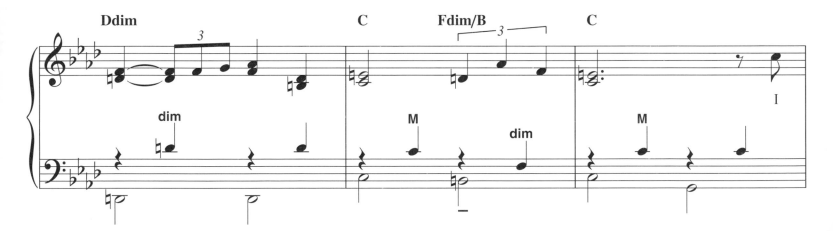

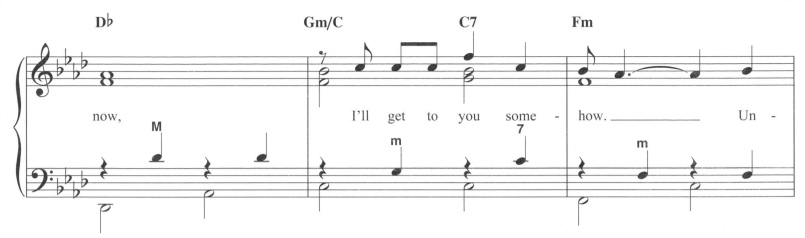

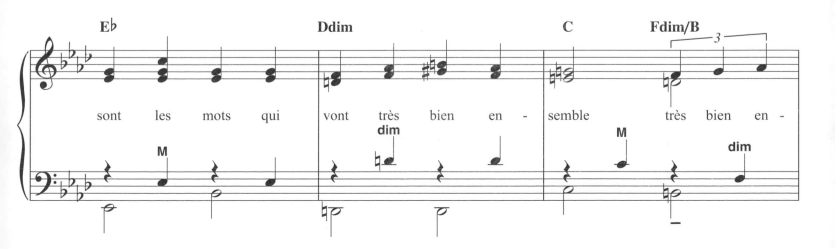

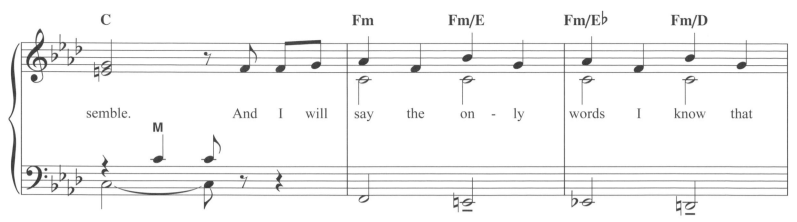

semble. And I will say the on - ly words I know that

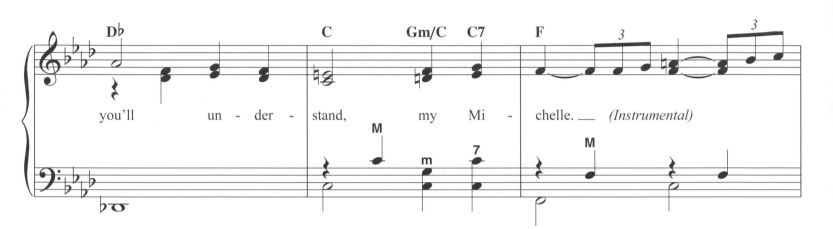

you'll un - der - stand, my Mi - chelle. ___ *(Instrumental)*

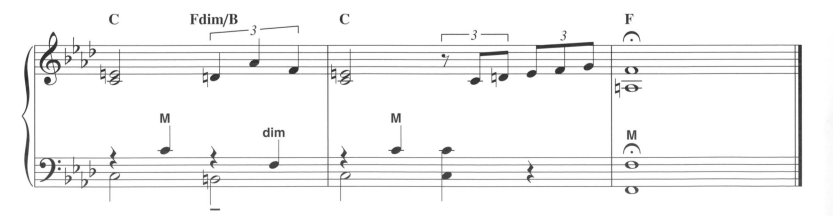

WHEN I'M SIXTY-FOUR

Words and Music by JOHN LENNON
and PAUL McCARTNEY

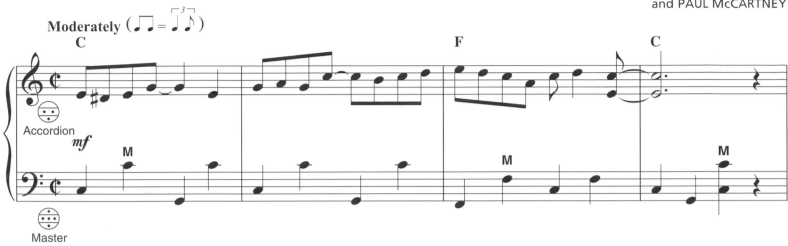

When I get old - er, los - ing my hair _

man - y years from now, _ will you still be send - ing me a

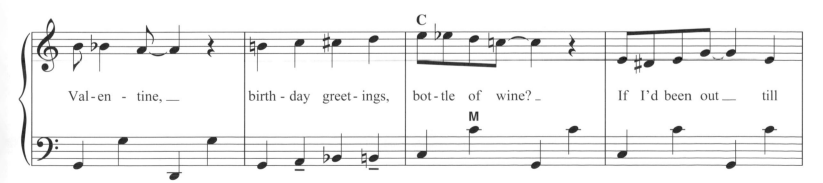

Val - en - tine, _ birth - day greet - ings, bot - tle of wine? _ If I'd been out _ till

quar-ter to three, _ would you lock the door? ____ Will you still need _ me,

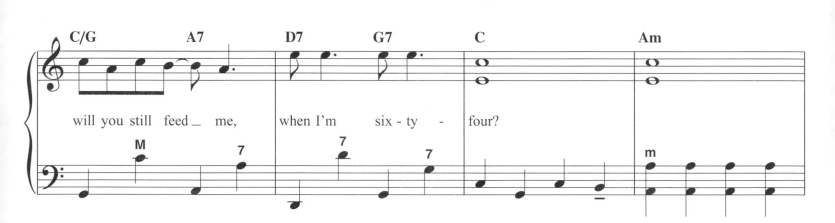

will you still feed _ me, when I'm six-ty - four?

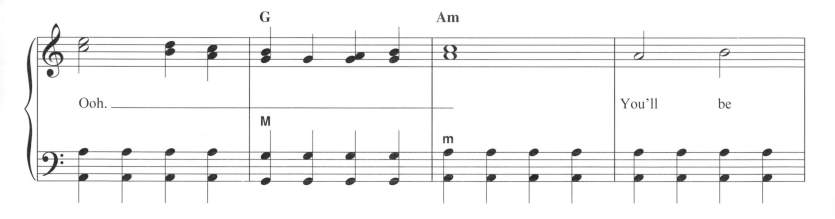

Ooh. _____ You'll be

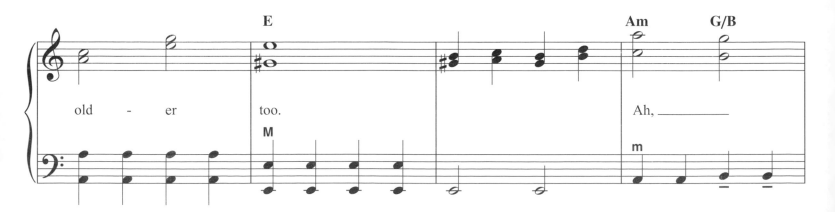

old - er too. Ah, _____

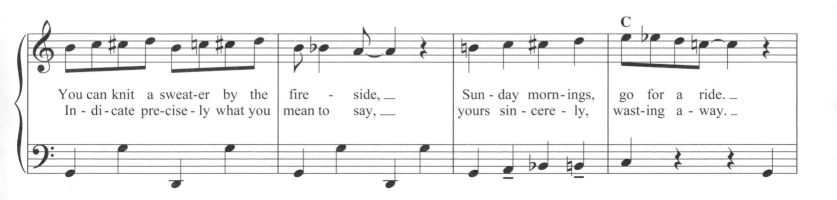

Doing the gar - den, dig-ging the weeds, __ who could ask for more? __
Give me your an - swer, fill in a form, __ mine for - ev - er - more. __

C♯dim/F♯ **C/G** **A7** **D7** **G7** **To Coda** **C**

Will you still need __ me, will you still feed __ me, when I'm six - ty - four?
Will you still need __ me, will you still feed __ me, when I'm six - ty -

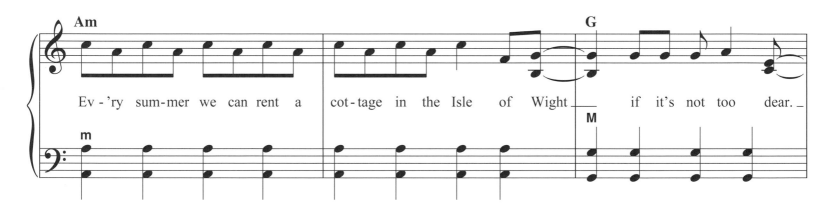

Am **G**

Ev - 'ry sum-mer we can rent a cot-tage in the Isle of Wight __ if it's not too dear. __

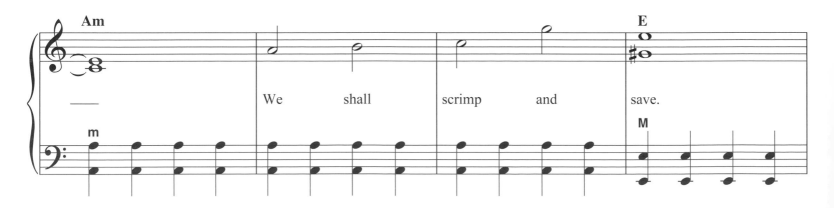

Am **E**

__ We shall scrimp and save.

OB-LA-DI, OB-LA-DA

Words and Music by JOHN LENNON
and PAUL McCARTNEY

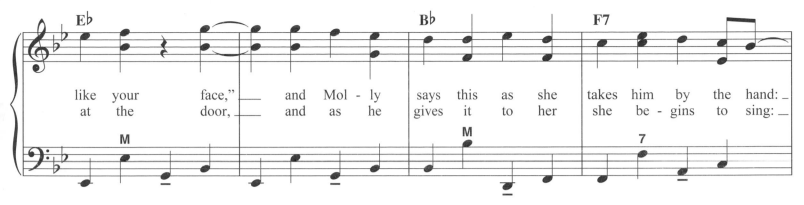

like your face," ___ and Mol - ly says this as she takes him by the hand: ___

at the door, ___ and as he gives it to her she be - gins to sing: ___

Ob - la - di, ___ Ob - la - da, ___ life goes on, ___

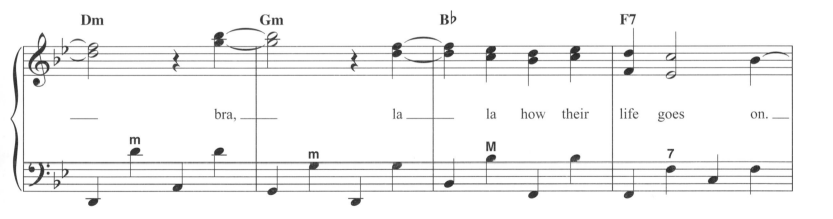

bra, ___ la ___ la how their life goes on. ___

Ob - la - di, ___ Ob - la - da, ___ life goes on, ___

52

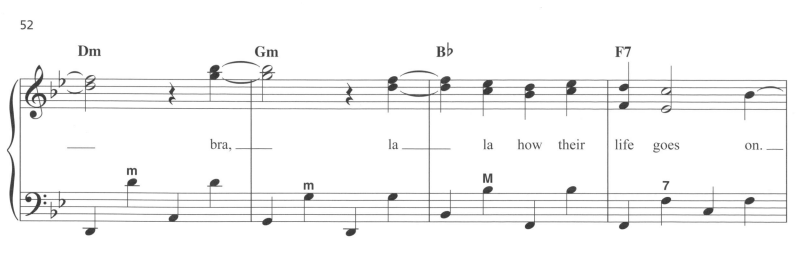

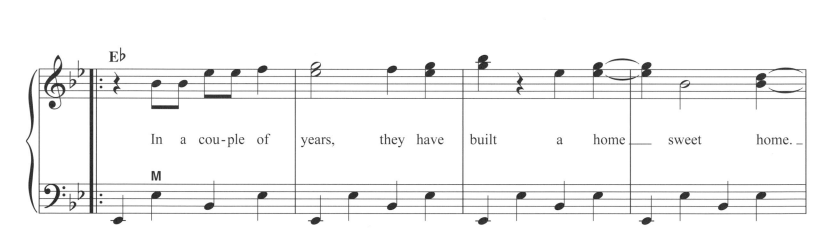

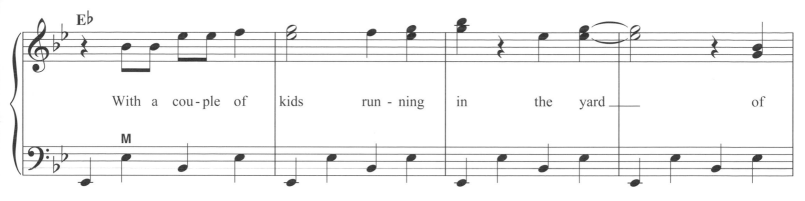

With a cou-ple of kids run-ning in the yard ___ of

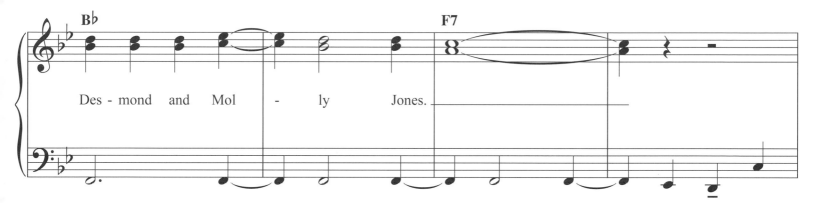

Des - mond and Mol - ly Jones. ___

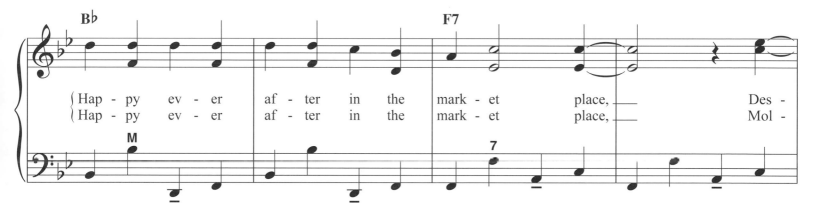

{ Hap - py ev - er af - ter in the mark - et place, ___ Des -
{ Hap - py ev - er af - ter in the mark - et place, ___ Mol -

- mond lets the chil - dren lend a hand. ___ Mol -
- ly lets the chil - dren lend a hand. ___ Des -

54

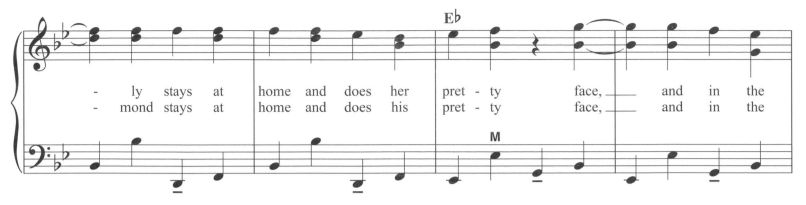

-ly stays at home and does her pret-ty face, ___ and in the
-mond stays at home and does his pret-ty face, ___ and in the

eve-ning she still sings it with the band. ___ Ob - la - di, ___
eve-ning she's a sing-er with the band. ___

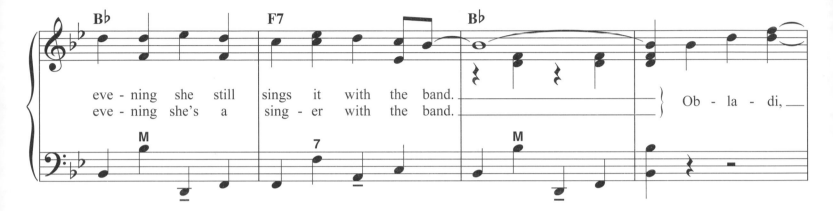

___ Ob - la - da, ___ life goes on, ___ bra, ___ la ___

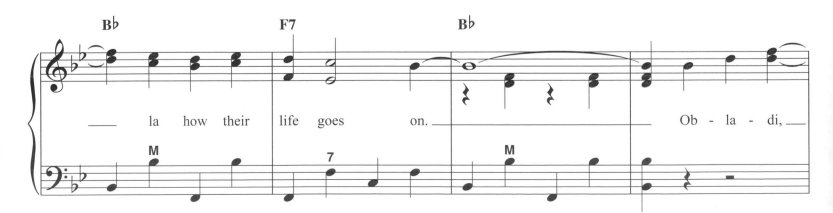

___ la how their life goes on. ___ Ob - la - di, ___

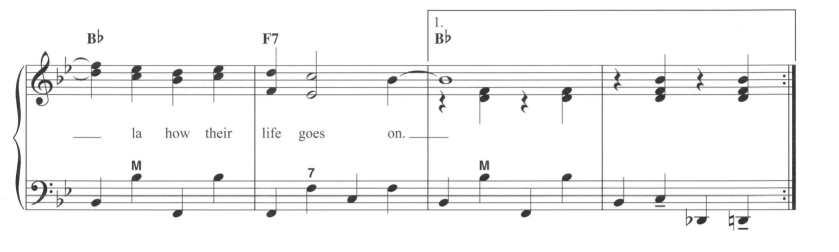

PENNY LANE

Words and Music by JOHN LENNON
and PAUL McCARTNEY

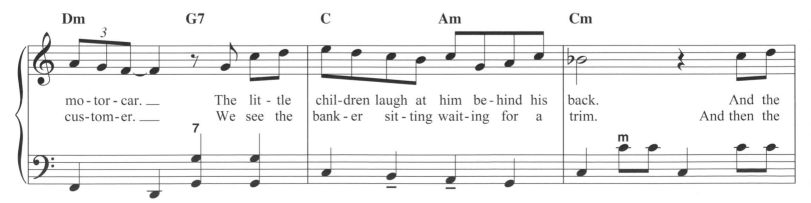

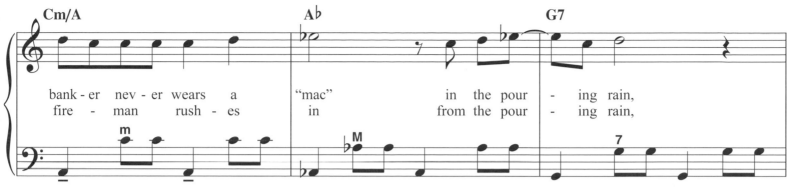

bank - er nev - er wears a "mac" in the pour - ing rain,
fire - man rush - es in from the pour - ing rain,

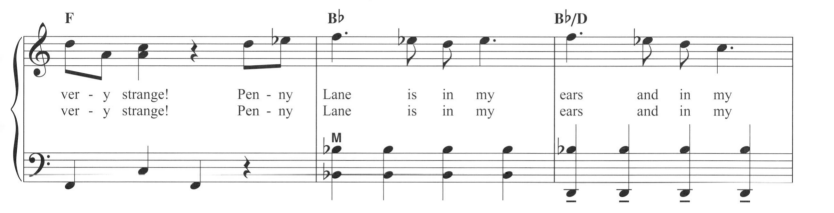

ver - y strange! Pen - ny Lane is in my ears and in my
ver - y strange! Pen - ny Lane is in my ears and in my

eyes, wet be - neath the
eyes, there be - neath the

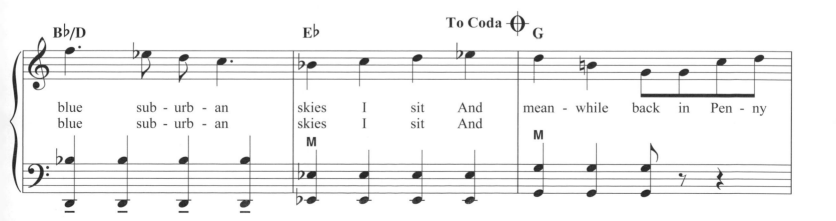

blue sub - urb - an skies I sit And mean - while back in Pen - ny
blue sub - urb - an skies I sit And

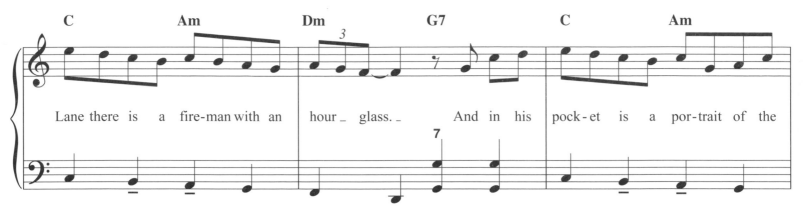

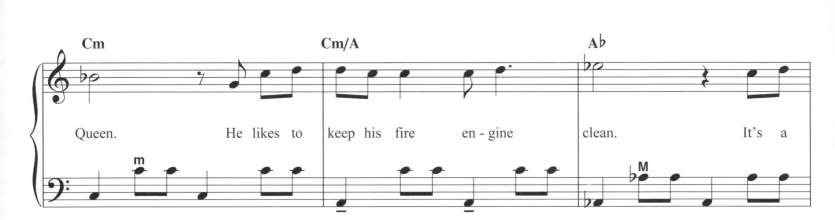

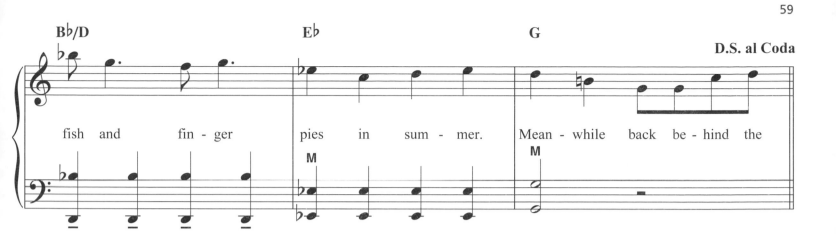

D.S. al Coda

fish and fin - ger pies in sum - mer. Mean - while back be - hind the

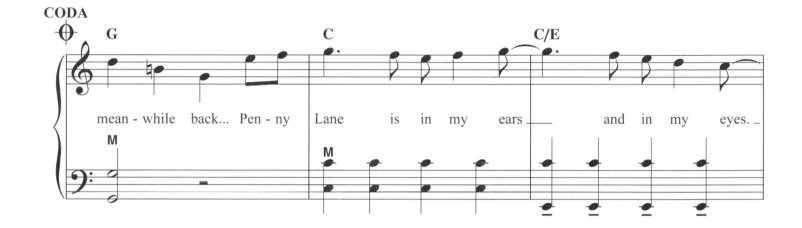

CODA

mean - while back... Pen - ny Lane is in my ears and in my eyes.

There be - neath the blue

sub - ur - ban skies. Pen - ny Lane.

YESTERDAY

Words and Music by JOHN LENNON
and PAUL McCARTNEY

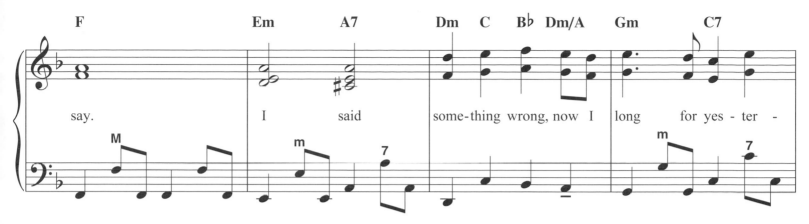

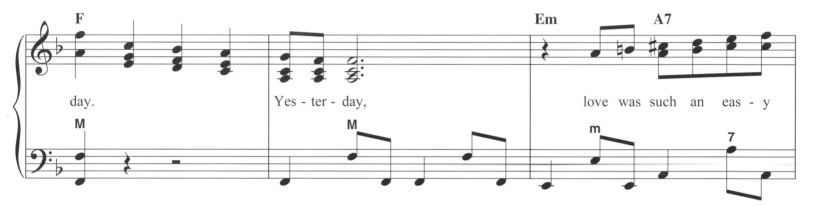

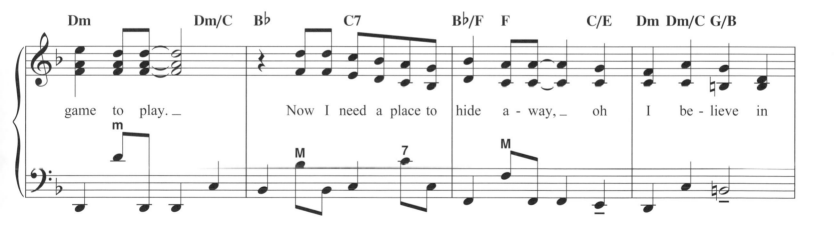

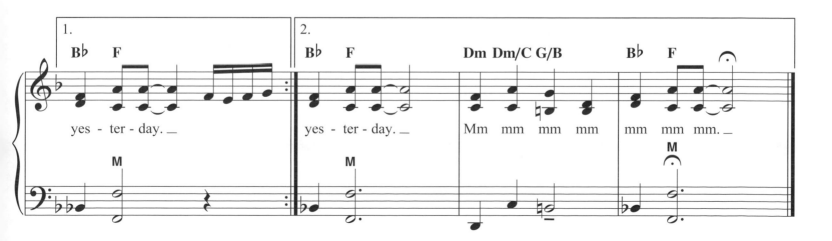

YELLOW SUBMARINE

Words and Music by JOHN LENNON
and PAUL McCARTNEY

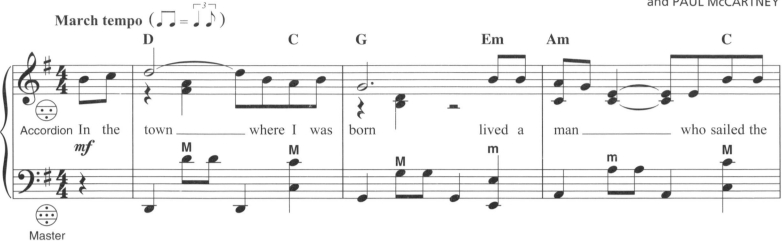

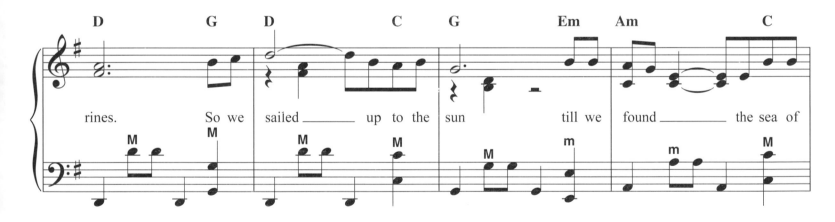

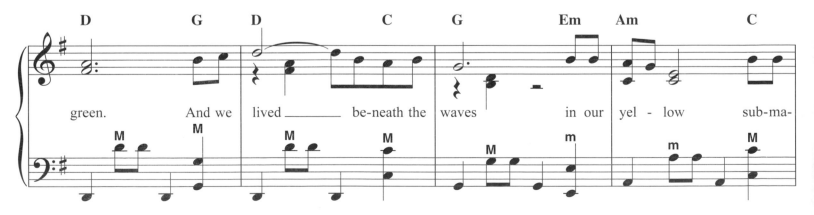

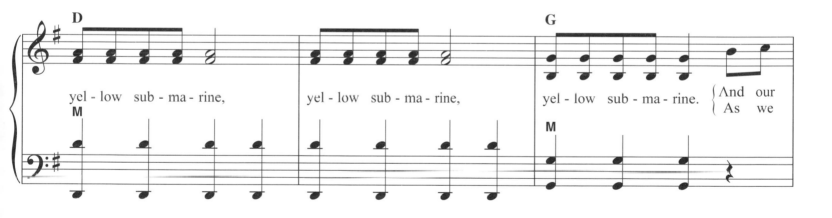

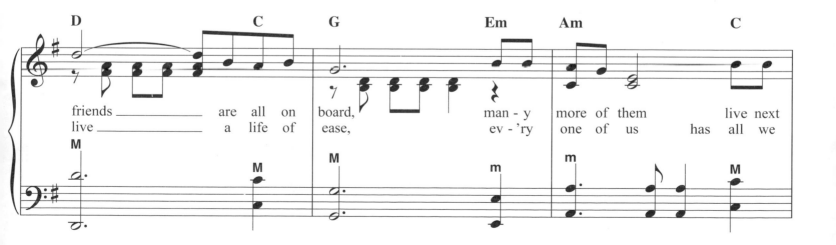

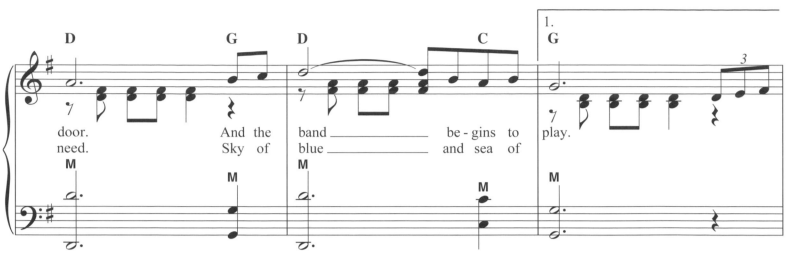

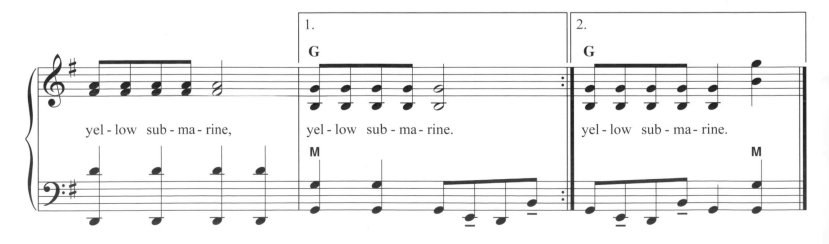